Big Bang
SCIENCE EXPERIMENTS

SUPER
SONIC
THE SCIENCE OF SOUND

Jay Hawkins

WINDMILL
BOOKS™

New York

Published in 2013 by Windmill Books, An Imprint of Rosen Publishing
29 East 21st Street, New York, NY 10010

First Edition

Editors: Joe Harris and Samantha Noonan
Illustrations: Andrew Painter
Step-by-Step Photography: Sally Henry and Trevor Cook
Science Consultant: Sean Connolly
Layout Design: Orwell Design

Picture Credits:
Cover: Corbis (Daniel Laflor)
Interiors: Science Photo Library: 4–5 (Steve Gschmeissner). Shutterstock: 8bl (Mikhail),
21bl (Rob Marmion).

Library of Congress Cataloging-in-Publication Data

Hawkins, Jay.
 Super sonic : the science of sound / by Jay Hawkins. — 1st ed.
     p. cm. — (Big bang science experiments)
 Includes index.
 ISBN 978-1-4777-0325-0 (library binding) — ISBN 978-1-4777-0370-0 (pbk.) — ISBN
978-1-4777-0371-7 (6-pack)
 1. Sound—Experiments—Juvenile literature. 2. Sound-waves—Experiments—Juvenile
literature. I. Title.
 QC225.5.H39 2013
 534.078—dc23
                                    2012026220

Printed in China

CPSIA Compliance Information: Batch #AW3102WM: For Further Information contact Windmill Books, New York, New York at 1-866-478-0556
SL002563US

CONTENTS

This book "sounds" like a lot of fun!

3

LISTEN HERE!

Is this the first photo sent back from an alien planet? No, it's a photograph of the inside of your ear, magnified 21,000 times! This book is full of facts and experiments exploring the science of sound.

GOOD VIBRATIONS

What is sound made of? It's a vibration that travels through the air, like the ripples that spread out when you drop a stone into a pond. When you clap your hands (or laugh, or burp) vibrations spread out in all directions, as air molecules bump into each other.

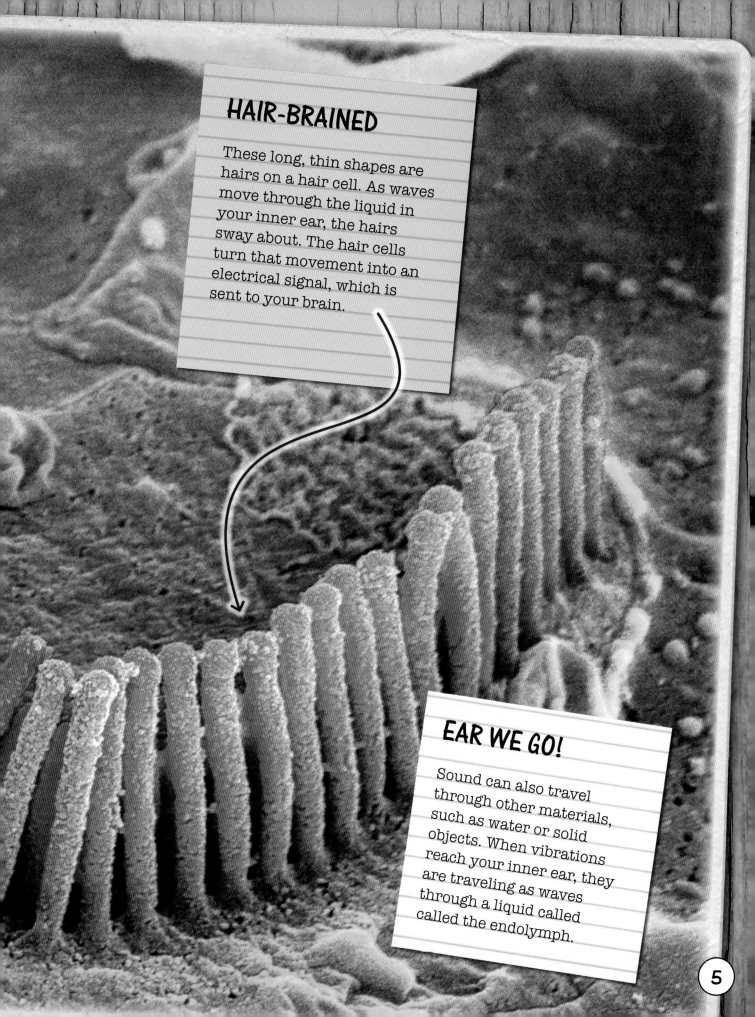

HAIR-BRAINED

These long, thin shapes are hairs on a hair cell. As waves move through the liquid in your inner ear, the hairs sway about. The hair cells turn that movement into an electrical signal, which is sent to your brain.

EAR WE GO!

Sound can also travel through other materials, such as water or solid objects. When vibrations reach your inner ear, they are traveling as waves through a liquid called called the endolymph.

MAKE YOUR OWN DRUM SET

March to the beat of your own drum with this noisy experiment. Using household objects, you can create a drum set that works just like the real thing!

YOU WILL NEED:

★ Containers such as small glass jars, cans, and plastic pails

★ Materials to make the drum skins, such as plastic shopping bags, paper, cloth, aluminum foil, and balloons

★ Materials to make drumsticks, such as chopsticks, cocktail sticks, and wooden spoons

★ A metal saucepan lid

★ Some string

★ Rubber bands

★ Marker pens

★ Scissors

★ Tape and a glue stick

★ Colorful paper

Which containers and drum skins work the best?

We robots love heavy metal!

Step 1

Draw around a can onto a plastic shopping bag. Then cut out the circle with scissors, adding a 0.5 inch (10 mm) margin around the edge.

Step 2

Stick the sheet in place with pieces of tape, pulling the skin tight as you go. Then decorate the can by gluing on colored paper.

You could decorate the drum with the name of your band!

Step 3

Test your first drum with two drumsticks!

Adding tape to the sticks will make a softer sound.

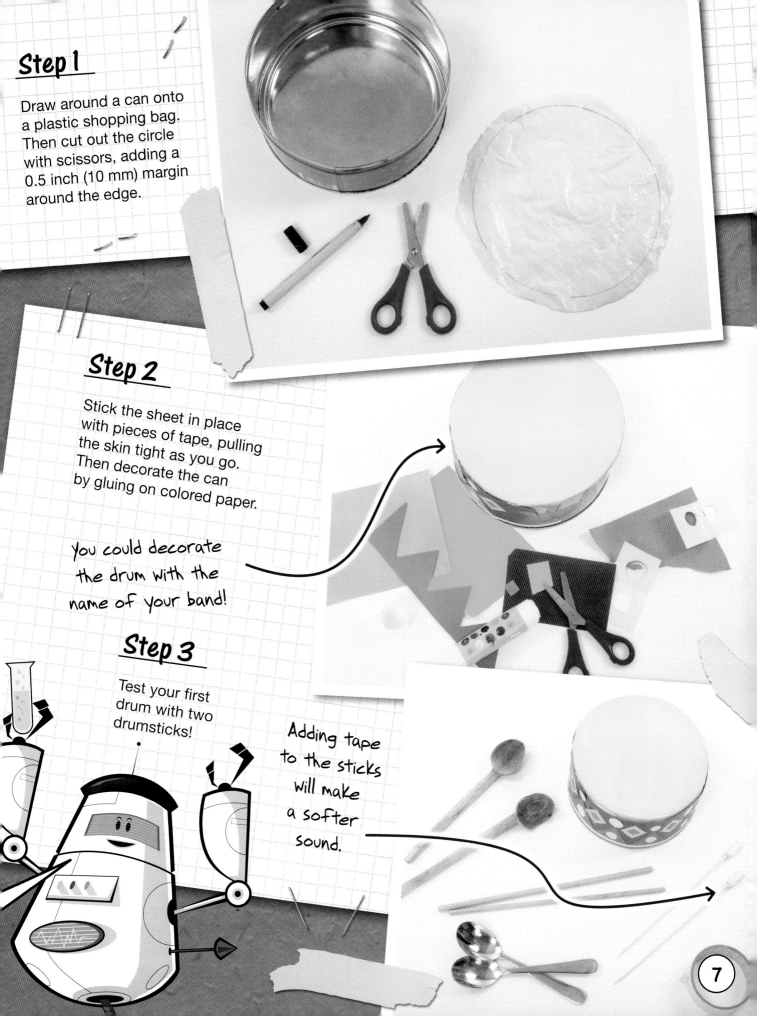

Step 4

Cut down one side of a balloon with a pair of scissors, to make a stretchy skin. Pull it over the top of a small container. Hold it in place with a rubber band.

The rubber band should be tight.

Step 5

Make some more drums from other materials. Each should sound slightly different. Finally, make a cymbal by tying a string around the knob on a saucepan lid. Hang it above the rest of your drum set.

Each drum in a professional drum kit is designed to make a different pattern of vibrations.

HOW DOES IT WORK?

When you hit a drum, it creates a vibration, which is what we hear as a noise. Lots of different things can change the pattern of the vibrations, which changes the noise that you hear: the materials you use, the size of the drum, how tight the skin is stretched, and even where you hit it.

DANCING FLAME

We all know you can make a flame flutter by blowing on it, but did you know that you can make a flame dance with the power of sound?

YOU WILL NEED:

* ★ A plastic bottle
* ★ Scissors
* ★ A plastic bag
* ★ A rubber band
* ★ A tea light candle and safety matches

Step 1

Using scissors, cut the bottom off a plastic bottle.

Step 2

Cut a square of plastic from a plastic bag that is at least 0.5 inches (10 mm) bigger than the base of the bottle. Fix it to the base with a rubber band.

Step 3

Light the candle. Position
the bottle so the neck
points toward the flame.

Step 4

Tap the plastic sheet
without moving the bottle.
The candle flame will
flicker with the sound!

HOW DOES IT WORK?

All sounds are vibrations in the
air. We don't normally see what is
happening when the air vibrates—
we just hear it as the vibrations
reach our ears.

However, the small flame in our
experiment is so sensitive to air
movement that we can clearly see
it move in response to vibrations
traveling through the air.

Very low-
pitched sounds
can blow out
flames!

GUITAR TABLE

YOU WILL NEED:
* ★ String
* ★ Scissors
* ★ A table
* ★ Four plastic bottles
* ★ Four pencils
* ★ Water

Have you ever wished you could be a rock star? You might not be able to take this instrument on tour with you, but it will show you how a guitar works.

Step 1

Cut two lengths of string, each twice as long as the top of the table.

Step 2

Fill two bottles with water. Half-fill another two. Then screw the stoppers on.

We're using the bottles of water as weights!

Step 3

Tie a full bottle to each end of one of the strings, and a half full one to each end of the other one.

Step 4

Arrange the bottles so the strings are stretched across the table.

The bottles will pull the strings taut.

Step 5

Put two pencils under each string, spaced at least 12 inches (30 cm) apart.

Step 6

Gently pluck each string in turn, between the pencils. Do they make the same sound, or is one higher than the other?

Step 7

What happens to the sound if you change the amount of water in the bottles? What happens if you use longer or shorter strings? Copy out this table and write down your results.

RESULTS TABLE		Higher or lower sound?
Heavier bottle…	with a longer string	
Heavier bottle…	with a shorter string	
Lighter bottle…	with a longer string	
Lighter bottle…	with a shorter string	

You've heard of rocking chairs. This is a rock and roll table!

In a real guitar, the sound of the vibrating string is made louder by the hollow space beneath.

HOW DOES IT WORK?

When you pluck the strings, they vibrate back and forth, making a sound. The vibrations will be faster and the sound higher if the string is taut.

SOUND CATCHER

Have you ever wished you had superhuman hearing? Find out how to make a simple device that can help you detect even the quietest sounds.

YOU WILL NEED:

★ A piece of thin cardboard measuring at least 16 x 12 inches (400 x 300 mm)

★ Masking tape or a stapler

★ Scissors

★ A friend

Step 1

Try catching a sound with your hand. Cup your hand and put it behind your ear like this.

Step 2

Close your eyes and ask a friend to talk quietly from about 20 feet (6 m) away. Try it with and without your hand. Does it make a difference?

Your hand is reflecting sound into your ear!

Step 3

Roll a piece of thin cardboard into a cone.

Then fix it with a square of masking tape or a stapler.

Make the hole about the size of a nickel.

Step 4

Trim both ends with a pair of scissors.

Step 5

Why not add some decorations?

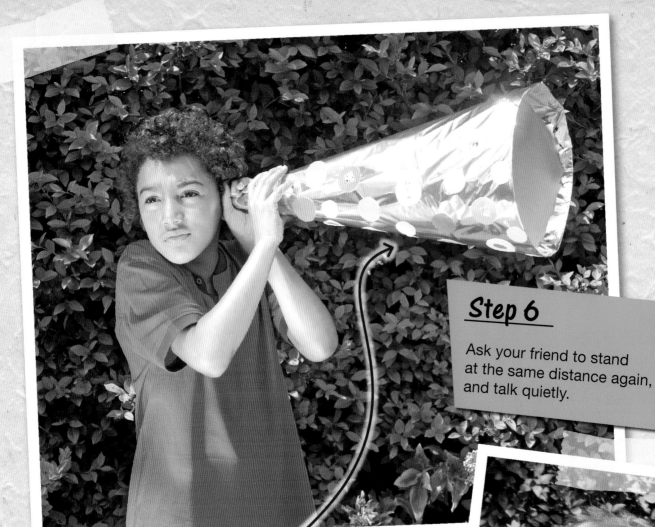

The bigger the sound catcher, the better you will hear!

Step 6

Ask your friend to stand at the same distance again, and talk quietly.

Step 7

How much better can you hear with the sound catcher than without?

HOW DOES IT WORK?

Our paper funnel catches sound from a wide area at its large end. That sound is then reflected down to the small end. This means that your ear is able to catch a lot more sound than usual.

What happens if you point the cone away from your friend?

PAPER POPPER

Who knew that a piece of paper could be so LOUD?

YOU WILL NEED:

★ A sheet of paper measuring 16 x 12 inches (400 x 300 mm)

Step 1

Fold the paper in half along the long side, then open it out again.

Step 2

Fold the corners into the crease line in the middle, like this.

Step 3

Fold it again along the original central crease.

Step 4

Fold the pointed ends together.

Step 5

Fold the top left corner down down like this.

Step 6

Turn it over, and fold the flap down in the same way on the other side.

If you folded up a sheet of music paper, would it play a tune?

Hold this end!

Step 7

The paper should look like this.

18

Step 8

Hold the noise maker like this.

Step 9

Swing the noise maker down like this. It should make a sound like cracking a whip!

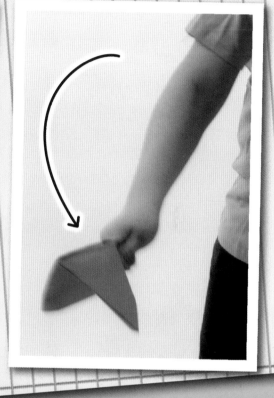

BANG!

HOW DOES IT WORK?

Swinging the noise maker downward compresses (squashes) the air inside it. The air is suddenly freed when the inner fold opens out. That causes a rapid decompression: a small explosion of air!

FUNKY BONE VIBRATIONS

We already know that vibrations can travel through air. They can also travel through other materials, such as... your head!

Step 1

Bang the fork on a table so that it makes a ringing noise.

Don't risk damaging an expensive table–any hard surface will do.

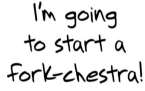

Step 2

Note how loud the noise is.

I'm going to start a fork-chestra!

Make sure you hold the pointy end away from you!

Step 3

Now bang the fork again. This time, hold it behind your ear, pressing it against the bone. Is it louder or quieter?

Step 4

Now bang the fork and grip the handle in your teeth. This time it should be really loud!

HOW DOES IT WORK?

This experiment shows you that sound travels better through bone than air. This is important because you have tiny little bones in your ear that vibrate, stimulating nerve signals to the brain to tell you that you are hearing something. If bone didn't conduct sound so well, you wouldn't be able to hear as well as you do.

WHERE'S THAT SOUND?

Why do we need two ears, and not just one? This fun experiment shows you why, by confusing your sense of hearing!

YOU WILL NEED:

★ Two pieces of plastic tubing about 20 inches (50 cm) long, from a hardware store.

★ Two funnels

★ Masking tape and scissors

★ A headband

★ An assistant

Step 1

Attach two funnels to pieces of plastic tubing. You might need to hold them in place with tape.

Step 2

Tape the two pieces of tubing together.

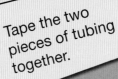

Step 3

Tape the tubes onto a headband.

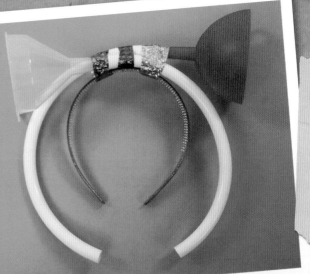

Step 4

Put the headset on your head, and hold the ends of the tubes, one in each ear.

Step 5

Close your eyes. Ask your assistant to make a variety of noises in different places.

The headset device confuses your brain by making it seem that your ears have swapped sides.

Step 6

Can you tell where each noise was coming from?

They will almost certainly get it wrong!

HOW DOES IT WORK?

We can normally tell whether a sound is to our left or right based on how loudly we hear it in each ear. The tubes take sounds to the wrong ears!

PAPER KAZOO

Here is how you can make the simplest, silliest instrument in the world. All you need is a piece of paper and some scissors!

Step 1

Rule a line on a piece of paper about 1 inch (2.5 cm) wide and about 4 inches (10 cm) long. Then cut the shape out with scissors.

Step 2

Fold the paper in half lengthwise.

Step 3

Fold the ends back like this.

Step 4

Using scissors, cut a small, V-shaped notch into the middle of the central fold.

Step 5

Hold it to your mouth like this and squeeze air between your lips.

Step 6

Try making longer and shorter kazoos! Does the sound change?

Step 7

Can you play a tune with your kazoos? Get your friends to join in!

Kazoos are named after the noise they make!

HOW DOES IT WORK?

Blowing between the two sheets of paper makes them vibrate and creates the buzzing sound that you can hear. Reed instruments such as saxophones and clarinets work in exactly the same way.

CUP SCREECH

YOU WILL NEED:

★ A piece of string about 15 inches (38 cm) long

★ A plastic cup

★ An old ballpoint pen

★ An eraser

★ Some water

This sound will make your hair stand on end!

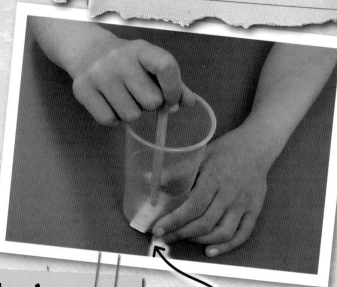

Step 1

Make a hole in the bottom of a plastic cup, using an old ballpoint pen.

Place the eraser under the cup to support it as you make the hole.

Step 2

Thread the string through the hole, and tie a knot in the end to stop it coming out.

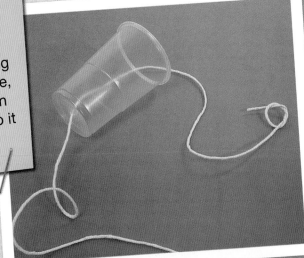

Step 3

Wet the string with water.

Step 4

Hold the cup in one hand like this.

Step 5

With your other hand, slide the wet string between your thumb and forefinger.

With a little practice, you should be able to make a horrible screeching sound!

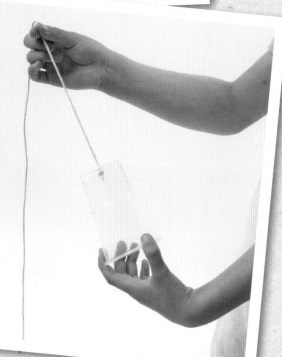

HOW DOES IT WORK?

Your fingers sliding across the wet string make it vibrate and the cup amplifies this, creating a screeching noise. Why do we find this screeching unpleasant? Some scientists think that it is because it is similar to the sound of a scream.

MAGIC RING

Gather your friends to watch you perform this awesome magic trick, made possible by the power of sound.

Step 1

Fill both glasses three quarters full of water.

Step 2

Gently rub a wet finger around the rim of each glass. With a little practice, you can make a strange, ringing sound.

Step 3

Adjust the amount of water in each glass until the pitch of the sound made by each glass is the same.

Step 4

When the pitch is the same in both glasses, place them together so they are close, but not touching.

ERROR! ERROR! This magic trick does not compute!

Step 5

Carefully balance a toothpick on the rim of one of the glasses.

Step 6

Wet your finger again and rub it round the rim of the other glass, making the ringing sound. The toothpick will move!

HOW DOES IT WORK?

Because the two glasses contain the same amount of water, they vibrate at the same frequency. Your rubbing creates vibrations, which cause one glass to ring and the other to vibrate and move the toothpick.

GLOSSARY

amplify (AM-pluh-fy) To make stronger or louder.

compress (kum-PRES) To force something into a smaller space.

conduct (kun-DUKT) To allow something to pass through more easily.

decompression (dee-kum-PREH-shun) The release of pressure on something.

detect (dih-TEKT) To discover the presence of something.

frequency (FREE-kwen-see) The amount of times something vibrates in a given period of time. The frequency of a sound tells us how fast its sound waves are vibrating.

funnel (FUH-nul) A cone-shaped object with a hole at the pointed end, allowing materials to be poured in a narrow flow.

magnify (MAG-nuh-fy) To make something seem greater. A sound can be magnified just as an image can be with a telescope.

molecule (MAH-lih-kyool) A group of atoms bonded together to form what is known as a chemical compound. A molecule is the smallest particle that still has all of the chemical properties of a substance.

nerves (NERVZ) Fibers in the body that transmit signals and sensations to the brain or spinal cord.

pitch (PICH) The quality of a sound dictated by the number of vibrations it produces. We hear pitch as the highness or lowness of a sound.

pluck (PLUHK) To pull something like a guitar string very quickly and then let go of it, causing it to produce a sound.

stimulate (STIM-yoo-layt) To cause something to react more quickly or more strongly.

taut (TAWT) Pulled very tight, like a string in a tight knot.

tea light (TEE LYT) A small candle that sits in a round cover made of metal or plastic.

Oh, so THAT's what that word means!

Brasch, Nicolas. **Tricks of Sound and Light.** The Science Behind. Mankato, MN: Smart Apple Media, 2011.

Gardner, Robert. **Light, Sound, and Waves Science Fair Projects.** Berkeley Heights, NJ: Enslow Publishing, 2010.

Jankowski, Connie. **All About Light and Sound.** Mission: Science. North Mankato, MN: Compass Point Books, 2010.

Kessler, Colleen. **A Project Guide to Sound.** Physical Science Projects for Kids. Hockessin, DE: Mitchell Lane Publishers, 2011.

Sandall, Barbara R., and LaVerne Logan. **Light and Sound: Energy, Waves, and Motion.** Greensboro, NC: Mark Twain Media/Carson-Dellosa, 2010.

Silverman, Buffy. **The Amazing Facts About Sound.** Vero Beach, FL: Rourke Publishing Group, 2013.

Sohn, Emily. **Sound: Music to Your Ears.** Chicago, IL: Norwood House Press, 2011.

Woodford, Chris. **Experiments With Sound and Hearing.** Cool Science. New York: Gareth Stevens, 2010.

Websites

For web resources related to the subject of this book, go to: www.windmillbooks.com/weblinks and select this book's title.

INDEX